How To Stop Procrastinating

Simple and effective methods to get over any task easily and on time

© **Copyright 2019 - All rights reserved.**

The content contained within this book may not be reproduced, duplicated or transmitted without direct written permission from the author or the publisher.

Under no circumstances will any blame or legal responsibility be held against the publisher, or author, for any damages, reparation, or monetary loss due to the information contained within this book, either directly or indirectly.

Legal Notice:

This book is copyright protected. It is only for personal use. You cannot amend, distribute, sell, use, quote or paraphrase any part, or the content within this book, without the consent of the author or publisher.

Disclaimer Notice:

Please note the information contained within this document is for educational and entertainment purposes only. All effort has been executed to present accurate, up to date, reliable, complete information. No warranties of any kind are declared or implied. Readers acknowledge that the author is not engaging in the rendering of legal, financial, medical or professional advice. The content within this book has been derived from various sources. Please consult a licensed professional before attempting any techniques outlined in this book.

By reading this document, the reader agrees that under no circumstances is the author responsible for any losses, direct or indirect, that are incurred as a result of the use of information contained within this document, including, but not limited to, errors, omissions, or inaccuracies.

Table of Contents

Introduction

Chapter 1: The Psychology of Procrastination

   The Science Behind Procrastination

Chapter 2: Why We Procrastinate

   Reasons for Procrastinating

- Unclear goals
- Long-term rewards
- Making it a future-self problem
- Holding out for better
- Optimistic about future abilities
- Indecisiveness
- Feeling overwhelmed
- Anxiety
- Task aversion
- Perfectionism
- Fear of negative feedback
- Fear of failure
- Self-handicapping
- Self-sabotage
- Not believing in your success
- Lack of control
- Neurological issues
- Depression
- Lack of motivation
- Lack of energy
- Laziness
- Prioritizing current mood
- Lack of self-control
- Lack of drive
- Impulsivity
- Distractions
- Sensation seeking
- Rebellion
- Boredom

Chapter 3: Motivation and Why You are Lying to Yourself

   The Three Components of Procrastination

   Productivity as a Motivator

   Comparing Ourselves to Others

Chapter 4: Point of Action

    Our Choices

Chapter 5: What I Want to Do vs. What I Need to Do

Chapter 6: Consequences of Procrastination

    What to Do

        Take two minutes

Chapter 7: Planning and Preparation

    Time Management

Chapter 8: Shift Your Focus

    An Imperfect Start

Chapter 9: Routines

    How to Get the Best Out of Your Routines

Chapter 10: How to Remind Yourself without Feeling Under Attack

    From Reminder to Habit

    Triggers

    Setting Your Own Reminders

Chapter 11: Fear and Self-doubt - The Final Stumbling Block

Conclusion

References

Introduction

This book contains everything you need to know about procrastinating and why it is so hard for us to stop.

For as long as science can remember, humankind has procrastinated. The Ancient Greek word *akrasia* means to act against one's better judgement (Clear, 2018). What that essentially means is that you do something different than what you know you should do.

For example, washing dishes instead of going to the gym (much like you have been meaning to for the last six months). While doing the dishes is still an important task, it is currently not the task you should be focusing on.

There is an inherent, immediate gratification to washing the dishes: your kitchen is clean, and you feel good for completing a task that you most likely do not enjoy doing. On the other hand, going to the gym will not have any immediate effects that you notice, so you are less inclined to follow through with working out.

That is how procrastination flourishes, no matter what good intentions we may have, immediate gratification wins over potential future payoffs. Planning your future sounds awesome on paper, but when you start thinking about it too long it gets a little jumbled in your head and you put off what you know you need to do in order to reach that imagined future.

The following chapters will cover more in-depth discussions of why we procrastinate, how we can stop procrastinating, and how to recognize the signs that you are falling back into the procrastination trap.

Chapter 1: The Psychology of Procrastination

This chapter aims to help you understand what procrastination is, what triggers it, and what psychological issues it could be connected with.

Procrastination comes from the Latin word *cras,* which literally means "tomorrow." How often have we told ourselves "I'll do it tomorrow"? This is what procrastination is. Putting off for another time what could be done right now.

Get fit and eat healthy? Tomorrow. Start your own business? Tomorrow. There is a lot to do, so much research and paperwork. You'll do it tomorrow when you are better rested or when there is more time. There is a myriad of reasons that we can come up with to do things "tomorrow."

As such, because we plan things ahead of time, tomorrow becomes a much more important deal than we think. Initially, we think "just this one day" will not have such a great impact, but those days tend to stack quite drastically. We will end up falling into the habit of putting things off.

By setting goals, you are planning your future, imagining the things you want from the future, or imagining the way your life will be after you have reached these goals. They can be anything from losing weight to setting a meeting with your boss to negotiate a raise or promotion to whatever hobby you wish to turn into a full-time career or business.

Many of these future plans will not affect you immediately. There will be no immediate benefit for you in going after these goals. The only impact it will have, as far as you can see, is that you will have to give up eating the junk you like (if your goal is to lose weight) or need to spend some serious time taking notes, making lists, and budgeting (if your goal is to start your own business).

These are all goals that will come to fruition in the future. The tasks assigned to them will benefit us in the future, but not right now, which is why doing them feels like a drag.

Long ago when we were still hunter-gatherers running across the open plains after our dinner, or adversely, away from becoming something else's dinner, we lived in what is referred to as an immediate return environment.

What this means is that the actions that were taken had some form of immediate benefit. Hungry? Go hunt. Thirsty? Stop by the stream. The human brain was not designed to constantly face tasks that are difficult or otherwise terrifying. Hunting solves an immediate problem, and while it has an element of danger, it is essential for survival. We avoided tussling with wildlife unless it has an immediate pay-out (Martin, n.d.).

The immediate return environment lasted until humans realized they needed to plan for some form of future. Sometime after realizing that winter yielded little in terms of food, they had to adapt. They had to start hunting larger prey or hunting more frequently in the lead-up to the colder months. They had to start gathering grains, berries, and other vegetation that lasted longer than meat would. They adapted to the environment they were in and taught themselves, and their descendants, techniques that would ultimately set in motion the evolution of humankind.

The current predicament humans are faced with is not the immediate problems of the environment (predators, weather, etc.), instead the problems we face are of the future, ten, twenty, maybe fifty years from now.

As an example, you could be out with friends at a bar on a Friday evening, having a great time. However, in the back of your head you could be thinking about how the workday went. A band steps up on stage and your mind starts to wander: "These guys are great; I should never have given up learning the guitar. Maybe I can still learn. What if I hadn't given up, would I have been where they are now? Should I quit my job to devote myself to my dreams?"

The greatest distinction between an immediate return environment and a delayed return environment is rapid feedback. Living in an immediate return environment leads to immediate results, that is why animals do what they do. They see a predator, run away, and are safe to graze another day. They know that when they see the predator, they need to stress in order to escape. We have no such perk in the modern age.

Thousands of years ago, when we lived in the same kind of environment as animals, stress and anxiety were useful emotions. They provided the cues our brain needed to react in either fight or flight mode, allowing us to take immediate action to the present danger.

Wild animals rarely experience chronic stress because there were rarely chronic problems to induce said chronic stress (Clear, 2018).

Imagine, for example, a predator makes an appearance in your immediate environment. Your brain registers stress and the accompanying physiological changes. You run away and the stress is relieved.

This is how the human brain evolved to use anxiety and stress to its advantage. Anxiety was an emotion that protected humans in their environment. It is more effective in short-term situations and hasn't adapted well into our current delayed return environment. As a result, when we face anxiety related to an unpleasant task that will take longer than five minutes to solve, we lean into procrastination to protect us.

The Science Behind Procrastination

Our brain is like a drug addict: addicted to the dopamine produced by experiences that we find enjoyable. The higher the likelihood that a task will be pleasurable to us, the higher the likelihood that we will choose that task over any other. Our brains will actively seek out these types of tasks while actively ignoring those that have a less enjoyable reward.

The fact that we reward this behavior with dopamine means our brain will go after the next fix, regardless if there are other, more important tasks that lie ahead.

The human brain is wired to enjoy procrastination because the rewards are immediate and pleasurable when compared to the task that is being avoided. There is an ongoing struggle between the limbic system (the pleasure zone) and the prefrontal cortex (the planning zone) of the brain. When the limbic system wins, for however long, the result is procrastination.

Unfortunately, the limbic system is stronger than the prefrontal cortex. It is also fully developed from birth and runs without conscious thought. The limbic system controls mood, instinct, and emotions. This is the system in your brain that sends a signal to your hand to move it away from the open flame so that you do not hurt yourself. Similarly, it sends signals to avoid other unpleasant or dangerous tasks.

The prefrontal cortex is where planning and conscious choice take place and needs to be consciously activated. It is also the part that separates us from animals that run on instinct (as is required in the immediate return environment).

Due to the fact that the prefrontal cortex is the weaker part of our brain, the limbic system will succeed more frequently in taking over when temptation presents itself. However, when procrastination kicks in, those are not the only parts of the brain that come into play. The amygdala jumps into the fray with its automated emotional response (see lion, have stress). What follows is a buildup of anxiety to the point where the brain will essentially grind to a halt.

Not wanting to be viewed as lazy, those who procrastinate often respond to this emotional reaction by taking control and allowing the prefrontal cortex to dominate. Other times, if the emotional response is too severe and the person is overwhelmed, a fight (resistance to the task) or flight (ignoring the feelings) reaction is created, causing the limbic system to work harder for its fix. This is how the brain protects us against emotional environmental stimulants (Daftardar, 2018).

Chapter 2: Why We Procrastinate

Let's take a moment and look at the reasons behind why we procrastinate. Often, we are told to "just stop being lazy and do it." Are we actually just lazy, or is there a deeper, more complex reason behind this thing that plagues us?

Sure, there could be some element of truth to procrastination being a result of being lazy, however, most of the time it is much more complicated than that. We often do get lazy, but there is a big difference between procrastination and laziness (Burton, 2015).

Laziness is simply choosing to do something else, which in most cases seems easier or more pleasurable just because the *effort* involved in doing the main task is seemingly too much. While both laziness and procrastination have a lack of motivation as a factor, the main difference between the two is that procrastination has the general intention of completing the important task (because we want to, except there are a lot of factors involved in it and, oh, look a puppy!) and being driven to do so—just in a slightly delayed time frame.

There is a general consensus that it boils down to willpower, but in truth, procrastination has many causes, many sources, and can be overcome with different approaches. Understanding what causes procrastination will give you better insight into yourself and how you can adapt any tip found in this book (or elsewhere) to work for you.

Relying on self-control will only get you so far, simply due to the fact that there are many factors that affect how much energy (or willpower) we have to expend to restrict habits. The majority of the time, procrastinating isn't because the task we want to accomplish is hard or horrible, it is the anxiety build-up which causes us to pull away from the task that we have to do.

There is an inherent quality about the task that puts us off. *Something* that triggers a fight or flight response, causing us to put it off until the very last moment when we have pushed ourselves into a corner.

While not necessarily a large part of procrastination, some people find it difficult to let go of the idea that the task in question needs to be completed as near to perfection as possible. They want to do the best work possible and tend to get lost in the smaller details and end up losing a lot of time. Many other people see this as being lazy, however.

The trick here is that, yes, you want to put out good work, or even excellent work, but you also need to *actually* put out the work.

You cannot keep doing research for your business without taking the step forward and actually doing it.

You can plan your meals and gym schedules as much as you want, but you will need to actually set foot in a gym and start or it will never get done. Spending too much time attempting perfection when, most of the time it is not really required, will cause you to stagnate and keep putting off the task because it seems so daunting.

Too much planning needs to be tempered with a little abandon once in a while. Be careful, though! You cannot blunder ahead without at least a bit of planning, which is a symptom of procrastination as well. By having no clear goal, no guideline, or any form of planning you will end up chasing your tail (Kadavy, 2018).

As long as our own self-control and motivation outweigh the impact these negative factors have on us, we are able to work through bouts of procrastination. Conversely, when the effects of these negative factors outweigh our self-control, we will continue to procrastinate.

So, how *do* you find balance?

In order to beat procrastination, you will need to identify your own bad habits. Once you have figured out what it is that triggers your bout of procrastination, moving towards a solution becomes easy, or at least *easier*.

There are factors that come into play that make resisting procrastination that much harder. These vary from person to person and range from mental exhaustion to having nothing to show for the effort already put in to reaching your goal.

Our self-control is not unlimited. Anything that will push the effects of negative factors closer to the surface will make it easier to give into procrastination. However, there are exceptions. For people who procrastinate to add a factor of excitement to the task, such as waiting until the night before to complete a paper that is worth 50% of your grade, the act of procrastination is not a hindrance in this case, but a tool to achieve their end-goal.

Reasons for Procrastinating

Procrastination is something we all struggle with, and it can be thwarted with the right tools. Finding out what causes you, as your own individual, to procrastinate is always the first step.

You can go through the list below and identify some of the factors that you can notice in yourself. As I said, knowing is the first battle won.

As a quick side note, should you feel that your procrastination lies much deeper than simply being stress-related, seek professional guidance. Never self-diagnose mental issues as this could be potentially harmful to your health and well-being.

Unclear goals

Unclear or vague goals will increase the likelihood of procrastination.

Goals such as starting your own business or getting in shape are still valid, but they are vague and undefined. You can change this to not only make the task more manageable (see chapter 7, 8, and 9), but also to make the goal seem more concrete.

Additionally, if your goal is improbable, such as making a million dollars before you're 40 and your birthday is 2 months away, procrastination is inevitable.

Long-term rewards

We are more likely to procrastinate because the rewards for completing this task are far in the future. Going to the gym today does not seem to have any reward for you right now, but if you keep at it, you'll have that hard, beach-ready body that you have always wanted.

Yet, we tend to focus instead on immediate gratification because the future is such an abstract concept, which is why we tend to delay doing tasks that we cannot see immediate rewards for. The exam may be weeks away and undoubtedly anyone would do better if they started studying early, but the consequence hasn't become an ever-present threat yet. So, they put it off until the night before the exam.

It is also important to note that if the long-term reward is low, or lower than expected, even leaving it until the night before will most likely not spur someone to do anything. The value lies in the reward and not the time it takes to complete a task. The same can be said for the punishment or consequences of failing to complete a task in the time frame.

If the punishment is far into the future, we will be just as unlikely to act as if the reward was far into the future.

Making it a future-self problem

People who use this form of procrastination do not view their future-self as a part of themselves. Whatever problems may arise out of neglecting to complete tasks becomes the future-self's problem.

They need to eat better and live a healthier lifestyle, but they view the consequences as too far away to impact them and thus disassociate, continuing with the bad behaviors that will affect their health.

In this way the present-self procrastinates because the future-self will deal with whatever problems crop up. Much in the same way they put off doing tasks because the rewards will not benefit them now but will benefit the future-self instead. They tend to treat the future-self as a rival and award them the same courtesies.

Holding out for better

This is exactly like it sounds. You hold back from doing something now because you are hoping that somewhere down the line something better will pop up of its own accord. People tend to avoid action, avoid expending energy on a task they feel they will not need to stick with because something better will come along, and they will need all their energy for that task. This type of mindset can and will easily lead to long-term procrastination.

Taking the exercise example again, someone might actively avoid starting any form of exercise (this includes going for walks or doing an at home workout) because they are planning to join a gym later. They will avoid starting towards their health goal because they feel they can be better prepared by starting off with exactly what they want. They often feel that they may not be able to switch to a different exercise plan midway through and thus hold out in order to set their plan in motion.

Unfortunately, people that use this form of procrastination rarely follow through. These are the "I'll do it Monday" people that miss their chance and instead of just doing it the minute they think of it. The following day they will fall right back into the cycle of "I missed my chance; I'll do it next Monday instead."

Optimistic about future abilities

This alludes to people being optimistic of their own ability to get tasks done at a later time in the future. This makes the person believe that the allotted amount of time they are given to complete a task is more than they need and will complete the task sooner.

"I have more than enough time."

A student may very well decide to start their assignment at a later date due to the fact that they are optimistic about the time given (I have two weeks for this assignment - that is more than enough time) and optimistic about their abilities to perform as they imagine they could (the topic is so easy, I could write it in one day if I have to and still ace it.)

They overestimate their own abilities to *do* the task and put off the work, regardless of this being a recurring theme for them. Chances are these people promise themselves that they will definitely do it tomorrow and next time they will start earlier.

Indecisiveness

We procrastinate because having to choose between two seemingly similar tasks with differing outcomes overwhelms us and we lack the ability to make a choice (see chapter 4 on choices we make). People who are prone to this type of procrastination are unable to complete tasks on time. They simply cannot decide on which course of action to take and end up stagnating as a result.

A simple example would be you putting off starting a diet or going to the gym because you are unsure which one to stick with. They all look promising. They all look like the perfect program for you and yet you know that you simply cannot draw them from a hat because what if you choose the wrong one?

Writing your own book is an exciting prospect, but with the seemingly large number of topics you can choose from, getting started is the hardest part of completing that task. You will overthink it.

There are factors at play here that you need to be aware of:

1. **Too many options!** The more you have to choose from, the harder it is to make a choice. There will be too many options for your brain to focus on, dissect, and decide on before it freezes up and shuts down.

2. **Too many similarities!** If the options you have are similar in value, the payout is similar, or the amount of effort that goes into completing the task is similar you are more likely to procrastinate about which option to go with first. This is especially true if they cannot be easily ranked according to importance or urgency.

3. **Too much pressure!** The biggest factor here is that the more important the task, the harder it is to make the choice. The bigger the consequences, the harder it is to make the decision. Due to this, putting off making a choice becomes the norm.

Constantly needing to make a choice drains your reserves, allowing you to default to bad behavior such as procrastination because you're too tired to focus at that exact moment. You'll likely decide that tomorrow will be a better day to tackle the task.

Procrastination allows you to replenish your reserves, however, constantly hesitating will make the reward of procrastination deplete much sooner, causing you to default to procrastination again.

Feeling overwhelmed

Being overwhelmed causes the human brain to attempt to protect itself, causing you to procrastinate. If the number of tasks that you have to get done are more than you can handle, the chances are greater that you will avoid all tasks until you have a better grasp of the situation. If you break a larger goal into smaller tasks, you could be overwhelmed by the sheer volume of tasks that result from it, instead of the daunting goal as a whole.

If your goal is to become a bodybuilder, you end up dividing that goal into smaller tasks such as deciding on a gym, picking an exercise program, choosing a meal plan, deciding if you need a coach or not, picking a date for your competition, determining the prerequisites to being allowed to enter a competition, etc. These are now just as overwhelming and daunting as the bigger goal.

Anxiety

Due to the way the human brain is wired, our default response to anxiety is to avoid it. Avoiding a task because it induces severe anxiety is what causes these types of procrastination. For example, if you always feel anxious doing your finances, you may end up putting it off until you are no longer able to put it off.

The drawback in this is that putting off the task can add to the existing levels of anxiety, causing so much more distress than there was at the offset. This is known as a feedback loop. You are anxious about a task, so you put it off. You now feel anxious about putting the task off and you procrastinate some more.

The feelings of anxiety do not go away until after the task has been completed, removing all sources of anxiety regarding starting and completing the task.

Task aversion

Making a dental appointment falls under this category. Many people avoid making phone calls to book appointments because the task itself is off-putting. You procrastinate as long as possible (some people avoid it altogether and have other people do it for them) in order to not have to deal with the task. The more you dislike doing something, the higher the chance of procrastination and avoidance is involved with said task.

It may not just be about disliking doing something (talking over the phone), it could also be remembering bad experiences (being hurt by the dentist that one time when you were a kid). The task you are avoiding could be boring, time consuming, or you could feel it is too difficult for the proposed reward.

Perfectionism

Perfectionism causes procrastination due to the need to have a task be completed perfectly. This type of procrastination has the person doing endless amounts of research or rewriting entire chapters at a time in order to get it "just right." People procrastinate because the risk of failure or making a small mistake is so high (in their own minds, certainly) that they put off doing it.

Trying to get a project to a level that you deem flawless only causes a lot of self-induced stress. You end up reworking the same project in an endless cycle, putting of publishing or opening up to peer review, even though it has been completed for weeks. Although it is reasonable to want to produce good-quality work, aiming for something that could quite possibly be unattainable is just an excuse to delay handing in your project.

It is important to note, however, that not all perfectionists will gravitate towards procrastination. In some cases, being a perfectionist will undoubtedly be the driving force to complete all the given tasks in a timely manner. Perfectionism, in this instance, is a good thing because there is no procrastination or desire to delay due to a perceived lack of flawlessness.

Fear of negative feedback

Being afraid of what others think is cause to procrastinate. Not publishing a book you have worked hard on because you are afraid of the potential negative feedback that could come from it is the core of this type of procrastination.

These fears are often exaggerated and unjustified. You could be afraid to publish due to perceived negative feedback being much greater than it could potentially be. You are imagining a future where nobody will like your book, or the critics will tear it apart. When, in fact, the more accurate response will most likely be less dramatic.

Fear of failure

Failing at certain things is simply a fact of life, and yet we find ourselves shying away from any task that could hold that potential for us. Further, the more important the task is to you, the more afraid you will be of failure.

As an example, you could be afraid that your home business will not take off, so you avoid starting on it or avoid making it available to the public. You tell yourself you are "fine tuning" it, and this is to avoid failing.

Having low self-esteem and suffering from self-doubt (see chapter 11) could compound on this fear. If you are prone to focusing on the negative aspects in any situation, you are also more prone to feel the fear associated with perceived failure.

Just as with perfectionism, fear of failure does not always necessitate turning to procrastination. In some cases, when you have all the tools at your disposal, being afraid of failing or screwing up serves as motivation to complete the tasks on time.

Be aware that perfectionism and fear of failure and negative feedback more often than not go hand-in-hand. They could, theoretically, be present at the same time, but they are independent of each other in the way they potentially affect our ability to resist procrastinating.

You could be confident in your ability to complete a task, but still procrastinate because you think people will react negatively to the end result. You could also still be afraid of failing, even if you are the only person ever to see the end result.

Self-handicapping

Not to be confused with self-sabotage, although the two have similar characteristics and reasoning. Those who use this method often use procrastination as an excuse for their failures, instead of them having the failure blamed on their abilities (or lack thereof).

Think of it as a scapegoat. For instance, you put off writing your report until the last minute. When you get the marks back and they are poor, you will safely blame it on the fact that you procrastinated and not because you did not understand the topic at hand.

Here, procrastination acts as a defense mechanism. If a person fails due to their own abilities, the lash back falls directly on them. If they fail due to procrastination or "running out of time," they blame it on that and avoid the negativity associated with that failure.

Self-sabotage

Self-sabotaging differs from self-handicapping in the way that these people firmly believe they are not worthy of being in a better position in life. They procrastinate looking for new opportunities because in their minds they are not worth the effort it takes to step out of their comfort zones (no matter how unhappy they are in that environment).

The reasons vary for why people engage in self-sabotage, but most notably those who procrastinate in this way are more likely to engage in other related behaviors such as pushing away those who wish to help.

Not believing in your success

Not believing in your own abilities to achieve your goals will cause you to fall onto the "safety" that is procrastination. If you are given a task that you do not think you can handle it will definitely cause you to put it off as long as possible. Chances are this is because you feel that you will most likely fail at the task anyway.

Many people have different levels of self-confidence when it comes to various domains in their lives. Someone who is excellent in presenting or talking in front of a large audience could have a lower self-efficacy when it comes to completing basic admin tasks. Self-efficacy is defined as belief in one's own abilities to complete a task successfully.

If you are an expert in your field, let's say you have been studying dinosaurs since you were five and this passion stuck with you and you are now a well-known paleontologist, your self-efficacy is high. Now add yourself into an environment where you feel out of place and uncertain, like a social event that requires you to mingle with people you have nothing in common with, your level drops like a rock.

This also means that if you are adept at something, your ability to self-regulate (control your behavior) is also higher, meaning you are more likely to finish tasks given to you that fall within your field of expertise. Conversely, you will be unable to self-regulate as effectively if you feel you will fail.

Lack of control

Procrastination is more likely to take place if you feel you have no control over your situation. As an example, you are more likely to procrastinate on a task if you feel that your efforts will be disregarded and criticized by your mom/boss/co-worker, no matter how much work you have put into it.

Control is experienced either internally, or externally (the locus of control or the location of self-control). While a perceived lack of control is individualized, it can be summed up as either of the following and you could land in either category, or anywhere between the two categories, depending on the task:

1. Those who are **internally oriented** feel that they have higher levels of control over their lives and choices. You feel validated, regardless of other people's thoughts about any aspect of your life and end up starting important tasks on time and completing them in a timely manner.

2. Those who are **externally oriented** feel that they have lower levels of control over their lives and choices. You feel that external factors govern your choices. Things like other people or things in your immediate environment control you. You value yourself only as others value you.

Neurological issues

Procrastination is seen as a personality defect, a sign that something must be wrong with them because you know what you must do but you cannot seem to do it. However, disorders like ADD, ADHD, Autism Spectrum Disorders such as Pathological Demand Avoidance, and depression all have roots in procrastination.

Largely, these conditions exist side by side and are near impossible to eliminate. Yes, there are medications and programs to help deal with the symptoms related to these neurological deviations, but some things such as Autism cannot be removed from a person.

Here we will take a deeper look into the neurological reasons behind procrastination—the reasons that are the catalyst that pushes some to procrastination either as a result of a disorder or as a means of coping with the disorder.

The biggest correlation that all of these deviations have in common is avoidance. Avoiding tasks that either aggravate feelings of depression or are a direct result (or symptom) of this neurological issue. It is important to note that avoidance is not a constant companion to these issues, but just like procrastination, it comes and goes depending on environmental input.

A common thought process for these kinds of people is that others who do not suffer from the same neurological issues seem to "have it together." They will feel that they are somehow worthless because they are incapable of "buckling down" to get things done. This neurological block can range anywhere from personal hygiene to visiting family to going out into public spaces and interacting with other people.

There are those who would seem to be able to manage the symptoms of their conditions rather well, but who still fall into an avoidance trap. They do not spend time procrastinating in complete avoidant bliss, but instead know that avoidance causes the anxiety and disruption in their lives.

Another cause behind this constant, uncontrollable avoidance could be attributed to underlying depression. Depression, as seen on the Autism spectrum, is more than just feelings of sadness. It is apathy and inertia (the inability to move) and recognizing depression as something other than sadness is still tricky to pin down accurately.

This is where certain psychological approaches could be combined with other methods in this book, such as cognitive behavioral therapy. It aims to change existing bad habits and behaviors as a way to not only help deal with things like depression, but also anxiety and procrastination.

The drawback in focusing on the small tasks designed to get the person moving is that it may seem pointless to those on the spectrum. Many people on the spectrum simply cannot handle being purposeless. Those on the spectrum find meaning in their own curiosity and interests and will struggle to find purpose in things that do not interest them. However, getting them to engage in research and following through on a learning experience about themselves and how they fit on the spectrum (as well as how avoidance is triggered) could help them reduce the duration of procrastination.

If you are on the spectrum, or you know someone who is, you may feel helpless when you try to figure out why you/they are procrastinating. From the perspective of someone who is not on the spectrum, this avoidance can be seen as an act of defiance or aggression. For example, you may ask your partner to take the trash out every Monday (the schedule never varies) and yet they still forget or seem to ignore the request. Be aware that it is not done on purpose (for the most part) and you can help them understand that there is a way to work towards a solution (Terra, 2013).

Additionally, in the case of Asperger's (part of Autism Spectrum Disorders), many who have this neurodivergence learn early on that it is much less stressful to simply avoid the problem instead of facing it. They believe the problem will eventually need tending to, as it will catch up, but for the moment the important part for them is that it will not be right now and that is perfectly fine. The typical response to feeling overwhelmed is to shut down and withdraw from the task (Uche, 2018).

A bit of a silly thing really, when you think about it, because avoidance does not solve problems (think deadlines, those things have a nasty habit of creeping up on you, don't they?).

As for those who have Attention Deficiency and Hyperactivity Disorder (ADHD) or Attention Deficiency Disorder (ADD), it could make starting, completing, or just sticking with tasks a real challenge due to the fact that their condition causes difficulties in concentration or focusing for extended periods of time. This is especially true if that task is a boring one.

They tend to go from task to task as they lose interest and never seem to be able to complete any of them. These behaviors often lead to procrastination, or they are seen as direct symptoms of ADD and ADHD. These actions of these types of procrastinators tend to be more associated with inattention and restlessness than hyperactivity.

Depression

This is sometimes a co-morbid problem, meaning it is combined with other mental difficulties such as discussed above. Most often, if depression is present, the typical feelings associated with it are treated, instead of on a case-to-case basis, as is required in this instance.

Procrastination due to underlying depression can lead to fatigue and reduced interest in activities once found enjoyable, and as such it will have them withdraw. The person who suffers from depression would be in no fit state to do chores such as cleaning up or laundry, let alone be mentally and physically energized enough to work towards their goals.

Lack of motivation

There is a whole chapter on this (see chapter 3), but it is worth quickly mentioning here. For the most part, people procrastinate because they feel they are not motivated to complete the task. They typically say things like "I don't feel like it" or "I won't be using this in the future, so why bother."

A student may put off completing an assignment that holds 50% of their end grade simply because it is not important for them to do well in that particular subject, regardless of the risk of failing. Although this should not be confused with a lack of control (locus of control and procrastination), there are both internal and external factors at work here just as there is for lack of control.

When an external force that drives the motivation is stronger than an internal one, the chance of procrastination is much higher. So, if your parents are forcing you to achieve higher goals such as getting straight A's, you are more inclined to procrastinate because those are not your goals. However, if you are the one deciding on setting the bar that high, meaning it is an internal motivator for you, you will be more inclined to follow through and not put off studying or completing important assignments and tasks.

Another important point to remember here is that one additional factor is also thrown in the works here. If you are an overachiever, you will be more motivated to do what it takes to reach your goals, regardless of external factors. The same cannot be said for those with lower levels of self-achievement. If you do not care either way, the chances of procrastination remain the same regardless of either external or internal forces.

Lack of energy

After a long day at work, you are more likely to put off tasks simply because you lack the physical or mental energy to complete the task at this time. Making a million decisions all day will also deplete energy which also leads to a greater chance of making the choice to avoid a task.

Laziness

Laziness is the unwillingness to act or to put in any form of effort required to complete a task. More often than not, laziness is seen as the reason behind procrastination. True, it has some effect and can definitely be a reason for procrastination, but it is not the only thing.

As an example, you need to wash laundry. It's been piling high for quite some time, and let's be honest, that smell is starting to get a little ripe. But you actively choose to leave it because you just don't want to do it.

Be aware that while laziness and lack of motivation can appear similar in some cases, they are indeed two separate issues that need to be approached and resolved as such. The trigger here is the unwillingness to act.

Laziness can also occur completely separately, regardless of motivation, drive, mood or perfectionism. A person can both be highly ambitious and lazy at the same time.

Prioritizing current mood

Whenever a choice is made on whether or not to act and take steps towards your goal, one of the "or" choices is to prioritize your current mood. This means instead of aiming towards a future goal, you focus instead on how you feel in the moment and make a choice to do something that will immediately improve it.

This form of procrastination is often hedonistic in nature and will end up being used to create immediate rewards for your actions and avoid the tasks that would draw away from the current pleasure return.

People who procrastinate in this way seek out activities that will be pleasurable in order to improve their mood. It may very well be something we all do, we call it self-care, and allowing it to get out of hand will cause a downwards spiral of seeking only immediate gratification. The future goal will be sacrificed for the current rewards.

Lack of self-control

Self-control, or lack thereof, and impulsivity have a habit of going hand in hand whenever we procrastinate. The two are not always linked, but more often than not one leads to the other.

Being able to control your urges is a sign that you are able to self-regulate your behavior. You are more likely to follow through and complete tasks when you are able to self-regulate. In the event of lacking self-control, you are subjected to making poor choices because you prefer and thrive off of immediate gratification.

Being able to control your urge to eat a whole tub of ice cream is more likely to allow you to be successful in your health goals. Adversely, should you lack self-control, even though you know what needs to be done, choosing to eat as much as you want (or sometimes more) delays the completion of your goals.

This is sometimes done subconsciously. The habit of giving in is so prevalent that there is no second thought given to stopping yourself when a situation such as this one arises.

We also tend to repeat "in a minute" as a sort of mantra or motivator when we are procrastinating. There is no reason for us to delay starting our tasks, and yet "in a minute" becomes hours of doing anything else because there is a lack of self-control.

Lower self-control shapes you in such a way that your future choices become centered around easy tasks and other choices that take very little effort or where the rewards outweigh the work.

At the same time, because self-control can become a mindless habit, we could end up spending hours doing something completely mindless such as scrolling through Instagram, even though it provides little to no pleasure anymore. We just keep doing it because we are incapable of self-regulating these bad behaviors.

Lack of drive

Having a driving force to guide you towards your goal is an immensely satisfying feeling. Being able to persevere and persist towards your goal, despite facing obstacles is what most of us strive for. Unfortunately, if there is no drive, there will be little chance of you completing the task even though you have already started it.

A good example is learning a new skill. Let's say you are learning to sculpt with clay. You are enjoying it; you have reached many little milestones and are progressing well. Then you reach a point where you feel you have mastered the level you are at and before actually trying to up the difficulty, you flake out and quit because the difficulty level seems too much for you.

There is no longer a drive to complete something because there are no more pleasurable rewards for doing what you are doing, and for you, these two are interlinked.

Impulsivity

Impulsivity is to act on a whim. It is to act without planning or consideration of consequences, rewards, or how it will affect those around you. Acting impulsively once in a while is fine. Acting out of impulse in order to put off a task is the building blocks of procrastination.

The act of procrastination is in and of itself an impulsive thing. It is to act without thinking of future consequences in order to do something *now*. Impulsivity feeds procrastination in that you could suddenly decide to attend a party instead of finishing the assignment you have been putting off.

Distractions

Distraction is the bane of productivity. Our lives are filled to the brim with things that distract us and being easily distractible makes focusing on one task at a time pretty impossible (sometimes these are symptoms of ADD and ADHD).

High levels of distractibility make you more prone to procrastinate. Instagram, Netflix, Hulu, Facebook, etc. are only some of the things that make it all too easy to be distracted.

However, it is also not the only way to become distracted. Some writers have hundreds of great story ideas throughout the week and will abandon a project they are working on to focus on the new idea. Rinse and repeat.

They are distracted by the thrill of the new idea and the new story that could become the next bestseller, but oh wait *what if this happened instead and we lived in a different universe?*

Sensation seeking

Thrill seekers. This style of procrastination is more often than not a personality trait. People procrastinate by waiting until the last minute to do anything because of the thrill it gives them. They are energized by the sudden rush of adrenaline.

If someone perceives a task to be boring and not worth their time, they could put it off until the very last minute to see if they could very well finish the 3000-word essay on the different uses of wood.

The result of this type of procrastination is motivation. Sure, the time you have to work is very little, but you are more motivated than ever to see if you *could actually* write 3000 words in an hour and still get a good grade. However, in most cases, this type of behavior leads to a lot of unnecessary additional stress.

Rebellion

Sometimes we resent the people who dole out the tasks. It could be your parents, your teachers, your colleagues, or your boss. We put off what they have tasked us to do, simply because we would like to avoid pleasing them in any way possible.

Often, if the relationships between you and the person to assigns the task isn't healthy, or open, procrastination becomes a way of coming with the negativity (Solving Procrastination, 2019).

Boredom

Procrastination and boredom are other things that are in close association. Some tasks simply do not challenge us in any way, either because the topic does not stimulate us or, compared to the things we actually want to do, it pales in comparison. So, in order to alleviate the boredom, you mindlessly surf internet sites, social media, or pick lint from your sweater (or a similarly mind-numbing task).

Procrastination can become a serious problem. Being bored affects the amount of effort you want to put into a task. It affects the willingness to start, and if left unchecked can spiral out of control and devolve into mindless and continuous procrastination.

The solution to boredom is quite obvious, however, following through is a little harder. The solution is to change the situation you find yourself in. Be mindful of when you procrastinate, and you can take small steps to change your habits.

The nature of this type of procrastination is being mindless in the moment. You will check social media due to boredom but end up wasting time and scrolling for hours. In order to help break yourself out of the cycle whenever the urge to return to a default setting occurs, such as mindlessly playing a mobile game all day, you can follow the following steps:

1. Take a deep breath.
2. Stand up and take a walk around your office, living room, kitchen, or if the space is too small, a quick walk to the front gate. Whatever your setup is, take a brisk walk. Move. The idea is to cause a shift in energy, to change your focus.
3. Take a couple more deep breaths as you walk or move around in your space.

There are also some questions you can ask yourself during this time to help ground you.

- How can I move away from the urge to procrastinate?
- How can I engage in the task I need to complete?
- I can make the right choices; will I decide to do so?

It is important to remember that you shouldn't be too hard on yourself. You are trying to change a habit that most likely took years to develop and it will take some time to break.

You are simply offering yourself the option to change your current situation and you may stumble, but that is okay too.

You can schedule some time specifically for you to procrastinate or just hang around doing nothing. Some people find it energizing to switch tasks in order to give themselves a short break and to relieve stress. Taking one step at a time is a surefire way to break out of the cycle (Essig, 2019).

Chapter 3: Motivation and Why You are Lying to Yourself

As a concept, motivation is a lie and here is why: motivation often comes after the work has started, not before. It seems a little paradoxical, doesn't it?

Unfortunately, we tend to wait around for motivation to strike. This is probably one of the biggest contributors to procrastination. We, as the human race, have been sucked into the lie that we need to feel ready in order to start a project or make that big change we want to see in our lives.

We wait for the right moment, wait for the moment when we will feel courageous enough, strong enough, confident enough to go ahead with our plans. Yet as we wait, we get more comfortable with the idea that we do not need to act because we will know when the time is right.

The human potential for greatness is nearly limitless. Look at everything we, as a species, have accomplished. Yet it is not with motivation that it was done. It was simply the desire to move forward, to grow, to build, and to be better.

Potential may be limitless but having all that potential is pretty useless if nothing is done with it. However, the human brain was not designed to do things that are difficult or terrifying. As the human brain developed and evolved over time, the core protection of the self is to avoid danger. Your brain is designed in such a way as to shy away from the things that could cause you potential harm. Unfortunately, in order to become a better person, or to reach your goals of becoming a successful business owner, you will need to push yourself to do the scary, uncertain things.

This is why we are often only motivated to do the things that are easy. Simply because it doesn't really need motivation. Doing easy things require little brain power, little risk, and almost no motivation. Buying a chocolate muffin with your morning coffee on the way to work is easy. Cutting the milk from your morning coffee is easy. Granted, it may taste horrid when you first try it, but it is still fairly easy.

Making coffee at home and packing food for the workday is a task that is not as easy as just popping in at your favorite coffee shop en route to work.

Why is it so hard to do the little things that are absolutely going to improve the way your life works? Because we focus on waiting for motivation. Waiting causes hesitation, which in turn causes doubt. When the thought occurs for us to act on our goals, there exists a small moment of hesitation right after that initial thought has crossed your mind. Everything hinges on this moment.

What we rarely notice is that that moment of hesitation sparks a primal response in our brain. It triggers a stress-response. You go through your daily life and your job fairly easily. You complete tasks, answer the phone, and converse in meetings without breaking a sweat. You are in and out of your boss's office on a daily basis to hand over paperwork and discuss the day-to-day tasks. Your brain has adapted and accepted that this is normal. It has adjusted, and thus there is no stress response to the things you are familiar with.

However, when you walk into your boss's office to negotiate a raise, you hesitate in the doorway. Just this once, that small act of hesitation triggers a fear response. Your brain picks up on it and send signals throughout your body that something is wrong. When you hesitate, red flags go off. So, with your heart is hammering in your throat, your brain starts talking you out of it. Here is where most people make their mistakes: they listen and walk away.

You know you are worthy of a raise. Whatever your reasoning, you should be able to discuss these things with your boss. However, because it is an act that you do not do every day, and because you imagine a negative outcome, you hesitate and back away. Live to fight another day, as they say.

There is no way of moving forward without making the hard decisions. Stop waiting until you are ready. Motivation only comes after you have already started, after you have already succeeded at something small. You are always one choice away from having a better life.

The Three Components of Procrastination

Our fears often make the decisions in our lives, such as the example above about the person who is unable to approach their boss for a raise due to the imagined negative outcome. Fear is holding them back so they will stand aside and wait for "a little motivation, a little more courage" before trying again.

Sometimes it takes one small step to create the change we want. Often, we hear "face your fears" but, in reality, it is actually closer to "face your problems." The problem you currently face isn't being afraid, it is you putting your goals and dreams off *because* of the fear. When you are scared, it is easier to point the finger to other people: "My boss isn't the easiest to talk to," or "I asked so-and-so to forward me the application, but I haven't gotten it yet."

These excuses make you feel better. Unfortunately, you will stagnate. Being overwhelmed by all the negative emotions and self-doubt cause you to fall back on procrastination because at this point, procrastination is your safety blanket. All the small decisions you make throughout the day are acts of procrastination: hitting the snooze button, cancelling on your friends, skipping the gym (just for today!). There is a gap between knowing what to do and doing it, but you just cannot seem to close the gap and actually do it. You make all these plans (these happen especially the night before, come on, don't lie, we've all been there) but they never come to fruition.

"Tomorrow I will get up earlier, and go for a run," or "tomorrow is the new me! I will be braver and work harder." Yes, at the point when you say these things you are completely motivated. You can feel it inside of you like a flame sparking to life, so much so that you *almost* consider not going to bed and then you realize "but it is so late already, I'll begin tomorrow." You are capable of so much, but you allow that little voice telling you that "it's like 11:22 p.m., man, can we just go to bed and do all of this tomorrow?"

Those few precious seconds you let your brain talk you out of your plans to achieve instant gratification mean that when tomorrow comes you will hit that snooze button again, because in that moment "just ten more minutes" is the instant gratification you are craving. However, you can outsmart your own brain and all it really boils down to is to break bad habits.

habit-loop exists in each of our brains and consists of three main parts: a cue, a routine, and a reward. These are the foundations of procrastination. These three, powerful words that become an obstacle in your path. By making a conscious choice to get up as soon as your alarm goes off breaks the routine, and breaks the pattern of behavior (Bilyeu, 2017).

Productivity as a Motivator

The best tip in order to be as productive as possible is to do the most important task first thing in the morning. It need not be the most difficult, but it has to be the most important.

Need to cash a cheque? Go do that. Wake up early and hoof it down to the bank. So completely simple, and yet, no one does it. But by doing the most important task at the beginning of each day, you will have a chain of incredibly successful days simply by acknowledging the fact that all important tasks have been completed for that week.

Productivity isn't about quantity; it is about quality. Getting the important things done consistently and early is what productivity is about. That is how productivity works. By doing the most important task first thing in the morning, then you'll get something important done every day.

You will notice that I consistently say, "in the morning." This is because our willpower and self-control are generally higher in the morning than any other time during the day. Although there are some exceptions, this is the general rule. Even though you may be a night owl and tend to get things done faster and better at night, this does not necessarily mean the task you're getting done at night is the most important.

You cannot back a cheque at night. You cannot phone businesses that do not operate 24 hours a day. Further, as your day progresses, other tasks could crop up that will cause a distraction. For example, you are tasked by your boss to bring her a cup of coffee on the way to work in the morning, so you do that first and put going to the bank off for a short while. After getting to the office your boss announces an impromptu meeting. Another hour passes by and that cheque is still tucked into the billfold of your wallet. So, the tiny tasks keep cropping up like weeds, putting the most important task out of your mind until tomorrow.

Unfinished tasks also tend to build higher levels of stress and anxiety within us, essentially guilt-tripping us because we made these plans and couldn't stick to them. Yes, that thin piece of fancy paper stuck in your billfold is judging you.

The best way is to be consistent with your tasks and thus build your productivity. Get a calendar and stick it to the fridge. For each day that you complete the most important task, mark off the day.

It doesn't have to be going to the bank. Your dream could be to be a prolific writer. In order to reach that goal, you will need to practice each day. Set that as your most important task for each day. Do it first, do it often, and motivation will follow. Notice that I mentioned nothing about writing well, it is simply about writing. The goal is to keep ticking those days.

Comparing Ourselves to Others

When we compare ourselves to others, we set ourselves up for failure. This style of thinking is becoming dangerously common: "If you can't be number one then you might as well not participate at all." Due to this, we become unmotivated to continue and end up throwing in the towel.

Instead of focusing on others, focus instead on giving it your all. Want to be a bodybuilder? Then bust your butt, put in the effort, and take your own risks. Do the best you can and push yourself to outshine only you. You will learn more by doing and practicing than obsessively studying other people. Achieving your goals are simply the product of willingness to try, regardless of the odds stacked against you.

Ask yourself these questions before thinking of how you compare to other people:

1. Are you willing to get in the gym and try it, even if you'll look stupid?
2. Are you willing to be vulnerable and start your own business?
3. Are you willing to improve your creative work?
4. Are you willing to suffer through mediocrity to reach greatness?

Take a risk and get started. Contribute something to your life, as long as you completed it through your own hard work and not by coasting of the coattails of another. Courage to get started is far more valuable than waiting around for motivation or planning for perfection without taking the step to reach your goal. Being perfect is not a prerequisite of happiness or success, stepping into the fray is.

Chapter 4: Point of Action

Here's the deal: you now have a quick background on the psychology behind procrastination. You have some scientific explanations as to why we procrastinate and what it really means to be motivated. During the course of this book, you will constantly come to terms with yourself and your own mind.

There are tons of blogs, videos, books, and other websites that tell you the "easy way" of getting through a bout of procrastination. What they do not always tell you, however, is that you need to ask yourself the biggest most important question right in the beginning: am I willing to put in the work to change my behavior?

It is all well and good that you want to stop procrastinating, but without the commitment you may as well grab a tub of Ben and Jerry's, kick off your shoes, and make "I'll start tomorrow" your new mantra.

These are undoubtedly hard words to hear. Even harder when you realize that the only person standing between you and your goal is you. Think of it as "tough love" and be brutally honest with yourself. Trust me, moving from procrastination to action could be the hardest thing you have to do. That is the Point of Action, or POA, that exact moment you decide to act. Most of the time these points are only reached due to extreme stress, either by the looming deadlines, a self-imposed guilt trip, or the fear of judgmental looks you get from family and friends.

Right now, you may not feel like going for a run. You may not "feel like" getting dressed and driving to the gym, but the point of action is the moment you decided to do it anyway. You get dressed, fill up your water bottle, and go to the gym.

Right now, you might be staring at that little black line blinking away on your blank screen, struggling to get words onto paper. The point of action is where you decide to write anything for two minutes. It can be a string of words or even just describing the way your coffee smells as it cools. You may have a creative block, but all it takes is to do *anything*, regardless of level of success.

The moment when you finally move beyond procrastination and act is what breaks you out of your procrastination loop. Knowing you need to write that book report yet putting it off until the last minute (ignoring the nagging little voice in your head) will bring future consequences to the here and now. Now, suddenly, the consequences of failing are hovering over you like a big, angry mama-bird. The pain of procrastinating finally reached that point where you moved from inaction to action (Clear, 2018).

You can break out of this cycle long before the future consequences become present consequences, all through your own choices.

Our Choices

We can create that point of action in our lives long before stress triggers it by the choices we make.

Every day we are exposed to millions of choices and outcomes. Sometimes one choice has a ripple effect that we cannot always see, while others are automated for the most part. We are bombarded by choices, from the clothes we choose for a meeting to what we eat to how we set up schedules, etc.

To us, making good choices reflects that we are living a rich, satisfying life. Which is why we continuously agonize over some choices more than others, more so when you take procrastination into consideration. Unfortunately, actually making a choice is inherently hard, since it means we will be giving up one thing for another. What scares us into inaction is that the thing we are giving up now may not be available for us to choose the next time (Ye, 2019).

So, what do we consider good choices? These are the decisions we make that push us in the direction you need to go. These kinds of choices reflect to the world around us that we are capable, smart, and valued members of society.

A bad choice, then, is one that negates this image we wish to project. A bad choice is counterproductive to what we have set out to achieve. As a whole, procrastination is seen in a bad light by society's standards. This conflict of interest normally causes stress, and in some cases confusion and despair.

Choosing something that pleases us in the short-term but has detrimental effects in the long-term is the root of this anxiety and stress we feel. While these choices seem harmless at first, and provide an immediate return of satisfaction, they will pull us away from our goal, one 10-minute snooze at a time.

The good choices we need to make in this situation are not what we want to do right now. These choices will give us future payoffs that we may not see right away but will reinforce the image we wish to project.

The biggest thing you need to keep in mind when you make choices is how they affect the important goals you have set out for yourself. If your goal is to become a bodybuilder, and you wish to dominate whatever division you are aiming for, making a choice that will hinder your progress is a bad one.

You may think that eating that slice of cake on your cheat day will not have repercussions beyond needing to work a bit harder the next day, when in fact, if you continuously make the choice to have a slice of cake on your cheat day, the effects will accumulate.

If one of your goals conflicts with the other, choices will need to be made. If your goal is to both be liked and accepted by your peers, as well as needing to be financially well-off later in life, attending an up-market event with said peers every weekend will negatively affect your goal to be financially well-off. Chances are that you will be spending large amounts of money before and during the event (think: new outfit or paying for tickets to attend said event). If you reject the invitation, you may negatively affect your relationships with those people. This is where you need to make tough decisions. Which of these goals is more important to you?

Understanding the way choices affect you both positively and negatively will allow you to make more informed choices. As with the example above, you know that achieving your goal of becoming a bodybuilder isn't going to be a walk in the park. Choosing behaviors that will make achieving that goal even harder is a choice that you will need to live with. However, when you are aware of which choices affect which goals in whatever way, you will be better suited to make the "good choice."

When we procrastinate the choice we have is either to do the work or to do another, more pleasurable task. When you know how these choices affect your goal, knowing which to choose is easy. Acting on those choices is where it becomes a little bit tricky.

Weigh your choices carefully and know which to choose. Knowing that your goal reflects who you wish to become, choosing the option that lines up with that ideal will provide you with a sense of security and certainty that you are moving in the right direction (Carey, 2015).

Chapter 5: What I Want to Do vs. What I Need to Do

Also known as "temptation bundling," this is the crucial part of making sure we veer away from procrastination. Basically, how it works is that you take the thing you really want to do (go play) and link it, or combine it in some way, to the thing that you have to do (write this book).

Most often, the thing you want to do is more instantly gratifying, like getting up to make coffee. It's really a small act, but it is an act of procrastination, nonetheless. By getting up, this seemingly harmless action will delay the task at hand (the one you need to do).

The longer you wait, the more tasks you will find in order to avoid what you need to do. One thing leads to another and then time has passed and now you think you might as well not do it at all because you have wasted so much time already. However, since you now know that you are procrastinating, you are in a position to do something about it, which is why the following exercise is important.

I want you to make a list, side-by-side, of the things you **want** to do and the things you **need** to do. You can use two sheets of paper or just write them down in two columns on the same sheet; whatever you want. As long as you can see, in big letters, the tasks that are fun next to the tasks that are not so fun.

Write down everything that you think is relevant. Heck, even the things you don't think are relevant, like getting up for another cup of coffee because the one you made an hour ago grew cold while you were doing "research."

This is known as "temptation bundling," a concept that is centered around behavioral research that simply suggests that you "bundle" together one task that is displeasurable with one task that you really enjoy. The idea is to take a long-term goal, such as losing weight, and combine it with a short-term goal, such as watching a new episode of your favorite show, in order to make the long-term goal more enjoyable (Clear, 2018).

For the next part, I want you to pick one **want** and one **need** and pair them together. Let's say you want to start your own business selling hand-crafted items. There is a lot of market research to do, financials to consider, budgets to draw up, and proposals to make. So, your **need** list would look something like this:

1. Market research

2. Make my product
3. Contact suppliers
4. Get a VAT registration number
5. Register the business
6. Hire employees
    a. How many and what would they do?
7. Packaging
8. Choose a courier company
9. Will I have a physical building? Do I rent or buy a property?
    a. Contact real estate agents
10. Design a website.
    a. Will it have an online shopping feature?

As you can see, these tasks are not always enjoyable. They aren't all that difficult, but they will take time. Time that you could use to spend with your family or friends, catch up on TV shows, or go out for dinner with your significant other. Some tasks are also limited to weekdays. If you have a steady 9-5 job as it is, getting these things done will be a challenge.

On the other hand, your **want** list will look something like this:

1. Watch a TV show
2. Garden
3. Go to the park
4. Bake cookies
5. Hang out at a coffee shop with friends
6. Go to a pub
7. Dinner with family
8. Attend a party
9. Read that new John Grisham novel

So, now it is time to bundle these tasks. For instance, you can get the John Grisham book in an audio format and listen to it while deciding on what kind of packaging to use to prepare your products for delivery. It will make the tediousness of color coding, pattern matching, and checking if your chosen courier company has limitations so much more bearable and the task will fly by much faster.

As you can see, some of these are easy to bundle together, and others are not. That is where they will turn into "reward points" instead. Attending a party or going to a pub will not combine well with the things that you need to do. In this instance, you will use a task from my **want** list, such as going to a party, as a reward for completing a task on your **need** list, such as finishing up the proposal to the bank.

There are consequences to our actions, good or bad. Temptation bundling goes hand-in-hand with avoiding consequences. The chapter that follows will cover it in greater detail, but the essence is to also use the **wants** of these bundles as a reward system in order to boost productivity and motivation.

Chapter 6: Consequences of Procrastination

Make the consequences of procrastination more immediate by also making the rewards more immediate. If there are immediate consequences, you will be more aware of the impact that procrastination has on your goals. Most of the time our goals are long-term, which means the consequences of avoidance are also long term. However, when we add in small rewards for reaching smaller milestones on the road to our bigger goals, we are more likely to stick with it and avoid procrastination.

Skipping one gym session will not have an immediate effect on you personally, however "buddying-up" will hold you accountable and make you look like a jerk if you skip the gym or fake an excuse to avoid going. The smaller reward here could be allowing yourself a scoop of your favorite ice cream at the end of the week if you consistently follow through with actually going to the gym.

We also need to take a closer look at why we tend to not take our own threats seriously. As with the example above, you can justify eating ice cream because you already skipped gym, you may as well finish the tub and restart tomorrow. If you are already flaking out on doing the task you need to, what will stop you from flaking out on punishing yourself for exactly that. It takes quite a lot of willpower to follow through, especially tasks that we find less pleasurable.

Whenever you put off doing anything it is because the satisfaction and enjoyment pay-out for that one task is much, much lower than whatever else it is you are doing at the moment. For instance, needing to load the dishwasher has little benefit to you right now, it is also unpleasant because it has interrupted your relaxation time after a long day at work, therefore you will leave it until the weekend because you are tired and need to relax.

When we say consequences, we immediately go to punishment. It is a negative outcome of an action, most often as a result of failing to do something or breaking societal rules. The consequence of putting off the task is dirty dishes all over the kitchen, weird smells emanating from the sink, and quite possibly a roach infestation. The immediate pay-off is more TV time. The long-term consequence is spending Saturday cleaning, disinfecting, and laying out roach traps. Time you could have spent doing more fun things.

Procrastination is a sort of avoidance mechanism in certain situations in order to cope with stress. You are putting off doing that spread sheet that your boss asked for due on Monday, because the stress of failing to complete that spreadsheet to your boss' specifications is pushing you to avoid the task altogether. Or it could be you putting off the gym until "tomorrow" because at this current moment, you are imagining what it would be like to actually do it—it takes effort, you need to concentrate, and, let's be honest, watching the newest season of Stranger Things is much more appealing than getting up and going for a run.

The effect of continuous procrastination is that you will keep putting it off in an endless cycle. The consequences being that the task is rushed, and your boss will be displeased by your performance or your next physical with your doctor will be more serious because your health has deteriorated.

Consequences are a part of the decisions we make. They can be good or bad. Instead of thinking of the negative consequences of putting off important tasks, flip the script and set out some rewards instead.

If you skip a workout, you will delay your weight loss goal, and if you skip out on a workout where you let your "buddy" down, you are letting your friend down. These are two negative viewpoints. Think instead of you going to the gym as holding your friend accountable to their own goals, in the sense that you are there to support them, and by not showing up you will let them down.

While both of these consequences hold the same weight, the one that has been changed to be seen in a more positive way will get the best results. This way you are more focused on the positive outcomes for completing tasks and not the negative ones. The types of thoughts you have will shape your reality (Diaz, n.d.).

Create a reward system, combining it with temptation bundling. You acknowledge that failing to complete the task will have consequences, and a reward system is you preemptively stopping the negative consequence and replacing it with a good thing. By making the benefits of your long-term goals seem more immediate, it becomes easier for you to keep going and avoid putting important tasks off.

There are other ways to allow the consequences of procrastination to have an immediate effect: you can use services such as *stickK*, a company that allows you to make a financial commitment to reaching your goals (one of the options they provide when you sign your personal commitment contract), with the caveat that should you fail to follow through, the money is lost.

For writers who struggle to stick to their daily word counts could use an app like *Writometer*. The app will not close unless your daily count has been met. This is also a good way to curb your social media scrolling. If you are interested, search through Google Play and download the app.

What to Do

If you still struggle with coming to terms with using "mental tricks" in order to achieve your goals because, honestly, smart phones are capable of running multiple apps at once and you can just minimize *Writometer* in the background and hop onto Instagram anyway. Instead, you can focus on using a commitment device in order to get you going.

Take two minutes

Whatever your goal, whatever the task you have to do, **take two minutes** to do it. We all know that if our end goal is to lose weight or prep for a bodybuilding competition, you will need to spend more than just two minutes a day in the gym, but the idea here is to simply start.

Even if you don't feel like studying, going to the gym, or reading that thick book your boss recommended to help you get that promotion, by spending just two minutes on it, you are, in fact, working towards your goal. Inefficiently, but we'll get to that in a bit.

Make the start meaningful enough to make an actual difference. At the same time, it needs to be simple enough to complete within the set timeframe.

You may have a goal of writing a book, thinking to set yourself a goal of 10 pages a day. While it seems doable at first, it certainly isn't sustainable unless you have already built the habit for it. You need to choose a task that is easy and sustainable but will also stack into long-term effects.

Researching ideas, plots, writing styles, and proper character building is a good task to have set each day, research will never finish the book for you. You will need to actually write. So, aim for something small like 500 words a day. Even if it doesn't fit in with the story, or there are things that make no sense, write. Clean up happens later (see chapter 8 for imperfect starts).

The same applies to fitness. Reading up on good posture or researching exercise routines is a simple task, but it is less meaningful than actually doing 30 squats each day, even if that is the only exercise you do all day.

You'll find that nearly any task can be fit into the **take two minutes** commitment device. The task needs to be as easy as possible to start. Anyone can walk down the road and back, read a page of a new book, or write one paragraph of their new novel.

So, what's the catch?

You only have two minutes. Go for a run, but only for two minutes, then stop. You *must* stop after two minutes. Go to the gym, but only do it for two minutes, then leave. It feels a little like cheating, but it works for exactly that reason (and if you think about it, skipping out on these measly two minutes is a little redundant).

It will feel silly, forced, and a waste of time in most cases, but that is the point. If you go to the gym for two minutes every day for two months, one day you will decide to stay a little later. You will decide that since you have to drive or commute to the gym each day anyway, why not make it worth it by staying 15 minutes or 30 minutes, or even an hour.

You are essentially building a new identity as someone who never misses a workout. You are only exercising for two minutes, so your goal isn't getting in shape. I mean, you could probably do two sets in that time, but it's rather inefficient and may be frustrating. This type of strategy works because you are setting the groundwork for consistency. You are setting the groundwork for developing a new habit. Duration isn't the point here, showing up and committing is.

You are taking small steps in the direction of your goal by cementing the type of person you want to be. How can you be a bodybuilder if you are not consistent with your workouts? It is better to do little bits than to do nothing at all.

Chapter 7: Planning and Preparation

Another commitment device we often overlook is pre-planning. By reducing the amount of effort you expend in needing to come up with a healthy dinner idea on the fly, if you have it pre-planned, all you really have to do is decide if you want to eat at the table or catch up on an episode of *Jeopardy!*

Plan your future actions, no matter the end goal. Again, if we want to become a bodybuilder, there is a lot to plan for. From gym schedules, to meal plans, to choosing which snacks are allowed. Start by writing up a shopping list and buy only what is on it (Clear, 2018).

Making decisions takes energy, and constantly making decisions drains willpower like nobody's business. Imagine pulling the plug on a tub of bathwater; it will drain slowly at first, but the more time passes, the quicker it goes. Constantly needing to choose the healthier of two options, like making a conscious effort to avoid social media to get work done, are decisions that drain your energy and willpower.

You may be able to resist pulling into McDonald's on your way home for a few days, maybe a week, but eventually your willpower will be at zero and you will switch to autopilot. This phenomenon is known as decision fatigue and it is a very real thing, which is why planning ahead will allow you to be more successful at reaching your goals and why limiting your choices will prove better in the long run.

We are often overwhelmed by choices. Walk into any grocery store, saunter down the breakfast cereal aisle, and just have a look around. The sheer amount of variation is enough to drive people insane. More so if you now have to read the food label because of your new diet. However, when it comes to needing to get things done (especially on a deadline), having too many choices available is not always a good thing. Having too many choices makes choosing harder.

If you had the choice between a red car and a blue car of the same make and model, the choice will be rather simple, maybe taking as long as five minutes. Add in extra colors and it gets a little more complicated, but still doable in a short amount of time. Now go ahead and throw in a couple of different models of the same make. Add in different extras, such as a metallic sheen, air conditioning, or built-in GPS. See what I'm getting at?

Restricting choices makes things easier. In chapter 6 we covered one such method (take two minutes), however, it can be adapted and applied to just about anything.

It is easier to write 100 words than it is to write 10 000. Starting small limits your choice but will make you more receptive to permanent change. Instead of focusing on wanting to finish that book you have been meaning to write since you were a kid, focus on finishing a character background. Write using only dialogue to describe a situation or limit yourself to using only 100 words to write a whole story.

If you want to start a new diet, start by eliminating a choice of take-out. Eventually, you will have eliminated all take-out and will only cook at home. Want to eat healthier? Add in just one extra type or color of vegetable.

We often believe that being able to choose whatever we want, whenever we want is what we need, but sometimes what is really needed is tunnel vision and as little choice as possible.

Time Management

Time management is a hard, but often necessary part of life. You will need to differentiate between what is urgent and what is important in order to prioritize. This is especially true when it comes to your health. We often disregard important tasks such as going to the gym as non-urgent when in fact it should be regarded as one of our highest priorities.

Going to the gym today is not urgent, but for your future health it is important. Same goes for eating healthier. Having a burger and fries won't hurt now, but down the line you may have other health issues to contend with due to overindulgence.

So, how do we go about utilizing our time effectively?

1. **Engage.** I want you to eliminate the occurrence of doing anything "half." This means needing to avoid distractions. It is incredibly easy to have your attention drawn away from the task at hand to just about anything else. That includes work tasks interrupting other work tasks.

Do not check your emails if you are busy writing a report. If you are on an important call, do not do anything else. Be fully present. Focus on the task you are currently doing. Regardless of how you get distracted or by what, it will take you twice as long to complete a task due to the occurrence of distraction. This is also why when we are on a deadline, we are at our most productive at the last minute because we focus hard on completing the task.

Think of how many more tasks are achievable if you eliminate the amount of distractions you subject yourself to. You can do this by:

    a. Setting aside time for each task.

    b. Not multitasking.

    c. Removing your phone and other non-essential technological items to a different room.

    d. Changing your location, such as going to a coffee shop if you are used to working from home but still get easily distracted.

    e. Doing the most important thing first.

2. **Stick to the schedule.** If this means you need to cut down on the amount of work you do, then so be it. Dividing tasks into smaller, more manageable chunks will help you stick to schedule and get things done.

Instead of allowing time and unplanned tasks to get in the way, use what is left of the time to stick to your schedule. If you set out to go for an hour jog, but due to unforeseen circumstances that time has now been reduced to 15 minutes, stick to it anyway. Instead of skipping your workout, do what you can with the time that is left. Do something today, even if it wasn't as much as you had planned.

Chapter 8: Shift Your Focus

Break down your tasks into smaller bits. Focusing too much on the larger picture will have you losing focus and reverting back to putting things off because the prospect seems too daunting.

As was briefly touched on in chapter 7, simply starting will help you set the ball rolling. You want to gym but lack motivation. So, start small. Just put your running shoes on. Then go outside. You don't need to drive to the gym, you can just go for a walk down the street. There's something in our brains that click on when we feel like we are cheating on action points. We think "I got dressed, ate healthy, and all I did was walk around the block? Let me walk around one or two more times to make the whole affair seem more worth it."

It is the uncertainty related to dreaming big that has got us stuck in a loop of anxiety/procrastination/relapse. Because we live in a delayed return environment (see chapter 1), we live in a state of uncertainty because we plan and think about the future.

So, how do we beat the system? How do we beat our stress-wired brains? The answer is simple: measuring.

Measure *something*. Since the future is undetermined, you can manage your stress-response by measuring something today. For example, you may not know exactly how much money you will have set aside for the day you retire (taxes, recession, cost of living going up, etc.), but what you can know is how much you are setting aside right now. You can deposit a small amount of money into a separate account earmarked specifically for retirement. That way you know at least you are doing *something* to prepare for the future.

The same applies to almost anything else in life. You cannot be certain that you will get top marks on the test, but you can study as hard as possible and do your best. You cannot know that you will marry one day, but you can go on a date and see how things go.

To be fair, measuring your small successes isn't some magical potion that will fix everything, but it is one way that you can take back control over your fear and anxiety. The discomfort we feel that causes procrastination is centered around uncertainty. The biggest barrier we face that ramps up the anxiety-procrastination trigger is simply starting a task. Wanting to lose weight is a good goal. However, needing to start, no matter how determined we may set out to be, will appear to us as a looming mountain.

Imagine standing at the base of a gigantic mountain, rock face as far as you can see. No way around and no way over. So, how do you move a mountain? One pebble at a time.

Shrink the tasks you need to do into smaller, manageable to-dos. It is easier for you to write a shopping list than to plan, cook, freeze, and buy a gym membership all in one day.

Often, we can eliminate the anxiety related to starting by conditioning ourselves to become used to the tasks. Habits require less brain power and cause less friction in our lives. By repeating the desirable behavior to the point it becomes a habit is the key to beating procrastination (see chapter 6 and 7 for forming habits).

Making your tasks more achievable is important because small measures of progress boost your confidence as you reach them, and completing these smaller tasks allows you to feel more productive and you will go through your task list at a much quicker pace (Clear, 2018).

Another way to shift your focus is to shift your mind away from what worries you to how you can prevent this future you dread. Instead of worrying about getting sick or having weight-related troubles later in life, go for a walk. Enjoy the scenery. Don't get hung up on the "get fit" part, focus instead on preventing the worry from returning.

Make it a small daily thing instead of this very large (and maybe a little scary) future prospect. The key to making this strategy work is making sure your daily routine not only rewards you immediately (immediate return environment), but also works towards achieving your future goals or solving your future problems (delayed return environment).

An Imperfect Start

With access to social media being readily available, and thus exposure to other people, it is easy to take inspiration from others. We see all of these successful people and try to follow their tips to become just as, if not more, successful. We try to reverse engineer and apply their tools to our lives in hopes of reaching as far upward as they have.

Sometimes it works, other times it is detrimental to your own growth. It is perfectly fine to learn from others and to be exposed to others' experiences enhance our learning curves. It is an entirely different thing, though, to copy from someone who has had years to perfect their own methods. You also run the risk of continuous comparison to others. You will measure your own success by someone else and thus feel incapable or incompetent because if you cannot do what they do (and they make it look so easy) then what is the point?

This causes you to believe that you need to have all these extra things in place before you can act. A common dream for many young adults is to travel the world, but the majority of the time they are held back by feeling ill-prepared or comparing themselves to stories and photos of others' travels.

You don't need the best equipment. You just need to start. It is true that the best gear and equipment can ease your travels, but it is not a must. It is nice to have a brand-new outfit for the gym, but simple shorts and a t-shirt will do.

The same goes for everything else you may set out to do. Starting a business, losing weight, learning a new language, etc. You do not need a fancy logo to succeed. You do not need to have a perfect website in order to start. You do not need new kitchen tools to eat healthier. You do not need organic food to eat healthier. Yes, it would be ideal, one day, to reach that level of optimization. But to start, just settle for cutting out junk food and adding vegetables to meals.

Don't get stuck focusing on the small details. We are so tempted to do our research on a topic that we get bogged down by the smallest of details and we get so hung up on needing to start perfectly that we put off starting because we feel we're not ready yet.

When you have decided you want to change, *that* is when you are ready. There is no perfect start, so do not be fooled by the cultivated perfection you see in the media. Imperfect starts can be updated, changed, and adapted as new information comes to light, as long as there is something to add to or change.

Chapter 9: Routines

Routines reduce the amount of brain power needed in order to stay on track. One of the biggest reasons for slipping back into old habits is the lack of a clearly defined system.

One of the best ways of staying consistent and on track is to follow these few steps. It not only provides you with a set routine you can follow on a working day, it also helps you remain productive in the workplace and reduces the chances you have to actively procrastinate.

1. At the end of each day, write down small tasks. These tasks are the six most important ones that need to be completed tomorrow. Again, this is about the level of importance not difficulty. Write down *only* six tasks.

2. Now prioritize those tasks in level of importance. Be honest.

3. When you arrive at work the next day, start with the first task on that list. Only concentrate on that task. Complete one before moving to another.

4. You can then continue working through the list in a similar fashion, spending enough time on the tasks at hand to complete them fully. Do no divide your attention by multitasking. Should a second, less important task pop up, complete the important one first before doing anything else. When you are done with the impromptu tasks, continue with your list.

5. At the end of each day, move any incomplete tasks on your list to a new list for tomorrow.

6. Repeat.

The fact that this is so simple is why it works so well. We often try to overcomplicate things with bells and whistles and forget that the idea behind this is to stay as organized as possible, in the most simple and efficient way possible.

Sure, there are other methods that you can utilize, but for the most part, this list can be adapted for just about anything that needs to be done, either at home or work.

You can also use this list to help you reach your goals. By adding the smaller tasks you need to do to the list as a part of the "important things," you will be able to work your way through the set tasks at a comfortable pace, with a reminder already in place.

There are critics who state that this method fails to completely account for the appearance of emergency tasks that could crop up, as well as other factors that could happen and derail our progress, but the simpler the better.

Not only does it force you to make tough decisions, it also forces you to prioritize those decisions. Having too many choices and too much to do can very easily cause you to become overwhelmed. That is why using this list helps you keep focus on the important things in your life. As new knowledge is gained, the list can be adapted.

There is also no friction in starting. The list has already done that for you. You know what needs to be done and it has been set out in a few easy steps the night before, leaving you to jump straight in as soon as you are up and ready. Starting is often hailed as the hardest part of getting things done and there is a great deal of truth in that, which is why giving yourself someplace to start will make starting just that much simpler. In the beginning, starting is better than success.

There is also no requirement to multitask. You are focused on one task and only one task. By prioritizing and doing only one task at a time, all your attention is focused on that one task, allowing for better, more consistent work.

Regardless of what method you use, if you use a piece of paper or some form of technology, the important part is to establish a routine by always doing the most important tasks first (Clear, 2018).

How to Get the Best Out of Your Routines

1. **Manage your energy better.** Time is relevant, but if you spend too much energy on a task that requires zero time to complete, you are wasting both time and energy on a task that could have been left or discarded. Alternatively, you may find that you are more suited to write in the evening, so set your schedule to reflect that instead of forcing yourself to write in the morning as soon as you are awake.

2. **Prepare the night before.** Do you remember your mom telling you to get your school stuff ready the night before? That was to reduce the time spent rushing to get things together right before you need to leave for school. If you spend a short at night planning your day, you will have a smoother start and feel more relaxed when getting into it.

3. **Do not open your email before noon.** Undoubtedly you have heard someone say something similar during the course of your life, but they have a point. If there is an actual emergency, someone will call. So, leave the email closed. It will also allow you to avoid being distracted by mindlessly scrolling through emails or hitting the refresh button a million times every ten minutes just for something to do. To avoid procrastination, keep that window closed.

4. **Turn off your phone.** Unless you are using it to do actual work right this second, put that thing away. Place it in a drawer or in another room of your house. Remove the temptation of going on to social media from your immediate environment.

5. **Temperature counts.** Working in a very hot room makes you slow and irritable. Conversely, working in a room that is too cold will also make you irritable. Your fingers will be stiff, your body will ache from being too cold, and your brain will draw constant attention to your discomfort.

6. **Move.** Your brain needs oxygen to function optimally, so get up and stretch. Walk around your desk or hop in place. Get blood and oxygen flowing to your brain.

7. **Avoid snacking mindlessly.** Set them as rewards for tasks completed. Not only will you feel more satisfied by completing tasks that come with a nice, yummy reward, if you choose a healthier option like yogurt instead of chocolate you will start feeling much better physically as well.

8. **Create a permanent starting point to your day**. Some people drink a cup of coffee, others meditate, while others read the paper. You can use this to set aside time for yourself. You can make it as long as you need. This small step triggers something in your brain that says, "Hey, time to get to work."

Chapter 10: How to Remind Yourself without Feeling Under Attack

There is a delicate line that we walk whenever we need to remind ourselves to act. There are moments where we know what we need to do, and we know what the consequences are, but we still struggle to get a move on.

Most of the time there is a little niggly feeling in the back of our heads, a small voice that nags us to get to the task at hand. We all know that one voice. Yet, we often choose to ignore it.

The act of ignoring that voice has the same effect as hitting the snooze button on your alarm. Ten minutes, but eventually the alarm will go off again. Except this time, it will be louder. If you keep hitting the snooze button, you will roll out of bed late, irritated, and just having an all-round horrible start to the day.

That is why reminders need to be as effective as possible and take as little time as possible to complete. These reminders that you set for yourself should definitely go hand in hand with the consequences that you have set for yourself.

Visual cues such as sticky notes in your workspace is one way to ensure you trigger the habit of working as well as a way to measure your progress. These types of visual cues are reminders that you will look at frequently, so place them at eye level. Stick them to the fridge, in the middle of the television screen, bathroom mirror, or anywhere you will walk past or look at during the course of your day.

If you are not too easily distracted by technology, there are apps available that will help as you can set alarms and milestones so that you cannot simply ignore them. Easy, right?

Unfortunately, if it were that simple, there would be no need for strategies to combat procrastination. The biggest turning point that needs to take place within yourself to be effective in your approach is to conquer your feelings. Our brains are wired in such a way that if you do not feel like doing something, chances are that you won't.

As an example, you know you need to go to the gym. It is one of your goals and you are determined. However, right now, you don't really *want* to...

That means that nine times out of ten, your feelings will win over what you know you need to do. You think to yourself if you don't feel like it, you won't be giving it your all anyway, so why bother?

A good place to start is the visual cue or physical reminder. Visual cues (no matter the format you decide on) are important for the following reasons:

- Visual cues act as a reminder. We often set goals that have not yet formed a permanent part of our behavior or routine, which is why, without a reminder, we will forget. We can be as adamant as we like, but once life throws a curveball and gets super busy, no amount of willpower will let you pass by the fast food place because you simply have no energy to cook, let alone cook healthy meals to aid in your weight loss goal. It is so much easier to stick to your goals if your environment works to nudge you in the right direction.

- A visual cue, such as a calendar, will provide you with a tool by which to measure your progress. It is satisfying to see each day ticked off as you go along.

- Having a visual cue will build your determination and get you fired up. The more progress you see, the better you will feel, and the better your motivation to continue (Clear, 2018).

No matter how well you set up your reminders and calendars, if you do not have an efficient and effective method for following through then you will not get things done. It is all perfectly fine to write up an extensive grocery list for your new diet, but it is useless if you forget it at home. Luckily for us, there are ways to ensure we remember the important things like taking that list with us to the grocery store (Robbins, 2018).

At the start we will need to push hard to remind ourselves constantly to follow through until we have reached the point where this new idea has integrated into our lives and become a habit.

From Reminder to Habit

A habit is an automatic action we take without conscious thought, such as making your morning cup of coffee or brushing your teeth. The act takes little to no conscious thought. Chances are everything from rolling out of bed to stirring in the sugar took no effort whatsoever. It is an action that you took because it is a habit. Most likely you have had the same morning routine for the last 10-20 years. The point here being that during the course of your daily life there are other actions that are similarly unconscious acts due to repetition.

However, there are habits that are bad, too. Browsing your Facebook page before hopping in the shower could take two hours instead of just a quick check in that it was meant to be. While building habits are hard, breaking them is even harder.

The good news is that once you have replaced the morning timewaster with a more productive behavior, such as packing a healthy lunch for work so that you do not buy a greasy burger instead because there wasn't enough time. This new, healthier habit will soon be just as hard to break as the old one. If you do things long enough, they tend to stick, and eventually the behaviors become automatic.

So, here's the trick: you will need to remind yourself often enough for it to become a habit. You need to find a way to interrupt your current action in order to trigger the new, desired behavior.

Triggers

Anything that draws your attention to remind you to do a certain task, such as doing the laundry or planning your gym schedule next week, is considered a trigger. You can sort the laundry and leave the piles in the hall or next to the washer. Someplace that is not out of the way, so that you cannot forget. Triggers and reminders are only effective if they work.

Set a timer or reminder on your phone to time your break so that you do not end up mindlessly scrolling through Facebook before work and end up being late. The new goal (to have a less rushed morning) is implemented by the new behavior (the timer) in order to break the old habit (hours of scrolling mindlessly through social media.)

In order to instill the habit, ensure that the trigger will interrupt your automatic processes. The drawback is that these require planning. You will need to remember to set the trigger to remember.

So, what do you do? Setting an alarm to get up earlier can be done beforehand and left to go off. That way you do not need to constantly remember to set an alarm to do so. You can place sticky notes on the fridge to remind you to be mindful of what you eat. It is mostly with one-off tasks that you would need to remember to set a reminder. The good news is that the majority of the time, triggers or reminders can be automated.

Setting Your Own Reminders

With the way technology is in this day and age, having access to apps that can help you set up automated triggers, is easier than ever. You can use your mobile phone, computer, tablet, etc. to set reminders to trigger behaviors.

Automated reminders build habits. Taking away the extra stress of needing to remember to remember, you can streamline the process of building your new habit that sets you on your future goal.

It is not only good for new behaviors, but also as a reminder for things that are too important to forget even as already established behaviors. Anything can happen to throw you off course, so automated reminders are ideal to cover you in case of a disruption.

Using your devices to set and send reminders is a great way to cover your bases. It may seem silly at first but setting a reminder to drink water or get up and stretch is the best way to fall into new habits. That way you do not need to worry about forgetting to do the things you want to do (Wax, 2019).

Chapter 11: Fear and Self-doubt - The Final Stumbling Block

Fear and self-doubt are constant companions to those who are prone to procrastination. In some cases, even to those who are not so prone to procrastination. These emotions affect how you feel and think about your dreams and goals and how you approach them. By allowing these emotions to control you, you will be at their mercy and you will avoid taking those first steps to reach your dreams.

Courage is not effortless, but it does become easier when we feel determined and driven to get what we want. Unfortunately, many excuses will surface because courage and determination are fleeting in the face of fear of the unknown.

These excuses justify sticking to existing bad habits, staying in a job you hate, or not going after your dream of owning your own business:

- The work does not challenge me.
- I am underappreciated, undervalued, or disrespected.
- I have no sense of purpose in my own life, so where would I go anyway if I were to quit.
- I need to study for a business degree.
- I have little money.
- I have no idea what I'm doing.

The list goes on. You can substitute those with any excuse you can think of. In some cases, the reasons seem quite justifiable, such as needing the job because you have bills to pay. However, they are still just that, excuses. They act as a safety blanket, so that you feel justified in staying exactly where you are.

The desire here isn't really the need for change or the need to reach a goal, it is to be *certain* of the path you wish to take. This is fear talking. Making decisions based on fear will hold you back. Your worries, concerns, and self-doubt control you. Unfortunately, the only result is that you do not do the things that are important to you.

We come up with as many excuses as there are dreams, often more, and we continue to let those thoughts keep us where we are.

"I want to gym and get fit, but I will look stupid running by myself," or "I have this idea for an awesome start-up business, but I want to be certain that it will work out before I quit my job."

Waiting on certainty is about as useful as waiting on motivation. When you go to the grocery store, how certain are you that you can navigate the isles, finding the things you buy every month? Chances are the whole trip is half done mindlessly. Since you know where everything is and you know what you are looking for, there is no doubt. This is because you have already done this task a million times.

Certainty does not necessitate starting, either. Think about moving to a new city. You don't really know the layout, but after some practice and getting used to the new environment, the area, the backroads, soon enough you are able to navigate the streets pretty well.

You will be forced to use a new supermarket for your grocery needs, but you still go even if you are unsure if they will stock your favorite brand of toothpaste. There was an element of uncertainty, maybe even a twinge of fear because of it, and yet you went.

The same applies to our goals. The majority of the time we want to feel motivated, energized, and certain about work, life, or other goals. We want to feel as though our lives have meaning and we are doing what really matters.

We want to be respected. We want to thrive. Yet, we settle for safe, even if some of those criteria are not met.

The good news is that you are capable of great change. You just need to give yourself a chance and stop waiting on the perfect moment. As stated earlier, an imperfect start is better than not starting at all (see chapter 8).

So, I have outlined a few ideas or thoughts that you need to keep in mind for yourself:

1. **Grant yourself permission to move forward.** If you are settling for something that is not what you want, give yourself the ability to change it.

2. Remind yourself that you are worth whatever it is you want to achieve.

3. **Start from where you are**. No athlete became the best straight out of the gate. They had to start somewhere, and so should you.

4. **Share your plans for change**. Share your plans with a close friend or partner. Sharing will help ground you and they can help hold you accountable. It is immensely powerful to own what you want by saying it aloud.

5. **Write down what you know**. Learn what you do not. You may not have a clear-cut idea of how you want to change, but you do know what makes you happy. This includes things you enjoy doing. Maybe it is helping out at the dog shelter every Saturday. It can be whatever you want, as long as it is yours.

6. **Do not let other people kill your fire**. Spend more time with people who build you up and cut out those who only tear you down. Go out and get in touch with others who share your drive. It does not need to be for the same reasons, the point is to increase exposure to what will be good for your soul.

7. **Take baby steps**. Sometimes we feel that the only way to reach our goals is to dive out of a plane and hope someone remembered to pack the parachute. Go at your own pace. The saying that life is a rat-race is for other people to worry about. You do you.

8. Keep breathing and moving forward (Essig, 2019).

One more thing that I want you to keep in mind:

Feeling silly or stupid is only because you are learning a new skill. Think of how a toddler learns to walk. They stumble, fall, wobble around, and we laugh at how silly they are, and yet they keep doing it until they can walk by themselves.

Be as fearless as the toddler. Even though we laugh at how silly they look, we never root for them to fail. Nobody is rooting for you to fail either, for the most part. If they are, it speaks more to their shortcomings than your attempts (Clear, 2018).

Failure is only certain if you decide to stop trying.

We can control the effort, but not the outcome. That being said, if you gave it your all and the result was short of what you expected, it does not mean you are a failure, it simply means that you reevaluate and try again (Shiffmann, 2016).

After all of that you may still feel self-doubt nesting in your head. You think to yourself, "I'm trying so hard, but maybe I'm not supposed to succeed at this," or "I want to enter a bodybuilding competition, but what if I can't cut it?" Self-doubt can be crippling. *If you listen to it.*

Getting around these stumbling blocks is easier than you think:

1. **Stop**. When these negative thoughts pop up, shut them down. Disrupt the negativity cycle.

2. **Talk to someone**. Often leaning on a close friend or loved one will help you deal with the negative emotions, and they can help offer some clarity.

3. **Don't compare**. You are succeeding at your own rate. Sure, you can draw inspiration from others, but do not fall into the trap of comparing yourself with others. Everyone moves at different speeds.

4. **People don't really care**. Worrying about what other people think about your dreams, plans, and actions you take to get there will do you no favors. Odds are, they're thinking about their own lives, plans, etc. anyway.

5. **Not everything is about you**. Did your boss snap at you or a co-worker give you the cold shoulder? They may be having their own bad days and, most of the time, don't mean to lash out. Think about how many times you flipped out at a family member because of stress.

6. **Setbacks are bound to happen**. The good news is they are only temporary. These are simply learning experiences.

7. **Prepare**. Worried about speaking in front of a large group of people? Hone your skills, do the research.

8. **Be kind to yourself**. Often, we are tempted to get mad and yell at ourselves for lack of motivation or repetitive bad behavior, but what works better sometimes is to be kind and offer constructive changes. Distracted by that new TV series? Instead of getting mad for wasting another day, limit the time spent watching TV. Hide the remote or whatever it takes to move you out of the rut.

9. **Celebrate your wins**, no matter how small.

10. **Come to terms with plans changing**. Forcing yourself to stick to something that isn't working is counterproductive. You are allowed to adjust your goals and approaches as you gain new knowledge (Edberg, 2019).

Conclusion

Procrastination can prove to be quite difficult to overcome and often people give up too easily. However, by taking into account each of the points covered in this book and applying them to your own life as strategies of overcoming your tendency to procrastinate, you will find that not only are you more successful at reducing the occurrence of procrastination, but you have a much better understanding as to why you are swamped with sudden urges to eat oodles of french fries while binge watching *Law and Order* for the seventh time.

The important thing to remember is that procrastination isn't some big evil thing that needs to be slain. Instead, think of it as a big, hairy dog that enjoys lying on your brand-new leather couch, chewing up your shoes—it just needs a little bit of training.

References

Bilyeu, T. (2017, January 31). *Mel Robbins on Why Motivation Is Garbage | Impact Theory* [Video file]. Retrieved from https://www.youtube.com/watch?v=LCHPS079rB4

Burton, N., M.D. (2015). What's the Difference Between Procrastination and Laziness? Retrieved from https://www.psychologytoday.com/intl/blog/hide-and-seek/201505/whats-the-difference-between-procrastination-and-laziness

Carey, T. (2015). Making Good Choices. Retrieved from https://www.psychologytoday.com/us/blog/in-control/201508/making-good-choices

Clear, J. (2018). Procrastination: A Brief Guide on How to Stop Procrastinating. Retrieved from https://jamesclear.com/procrastination

Clear, J. (2019). The Only Productivity Tip You'll Ever Need. Retrieved from https://jamesclear.com/productivity-tip

Daftardar, I. (2018). Why Do We Procrastinate? Retrieved from https://www.scienceabc.com/humans/shocking-origin-procrastination-biological-point-view.html

Diaz, C. (n.d.). Negative Thinking Versus Positive Thinking. Retrieved from https://www.the-benefits-of-positive-thinking.com/negative-thinking-versus-positive-thinking.html

Edberg, H. (2019). 13 Powerful Ways to Overcome Self-Doubt (So You Can Finally Move Forward in Life). Retrieved from https://www.positivityblog.com/overcome-self-doubt/

Essig, S. (2019). Procrastination and Boredom Go Hand-In-Hand: Flow-Dynamix. Retrieved from https://flow-dynamix.com/procrastination-and-boredom-go-hand-in-hand/

Kadavy, D. (2018). What's the difference between attention to detail & procrastination? Retrieved from https://medium.com/getting-art-done/whats-the-difference-between-attention-to-detail-procrastination-b20358149d0c

Martin, L. L., & Shirk, S. (n.d.). *Immediate-Return Societies: What Can They Tell Us About the Self and Social Relationships in Our Society?* [PDF]. Retrieved from https://pdfs.semanticscholar.org/0013/dd4dba80a0248656ecde6366eebb47fca938.pdf

Shiffmann, M. (2016). Why You Don't Need to Eliminate Self-Doubt and Fear. Retrieved from https://tinybuddha.com/blog/why-dont-need-eliminate-self-doubt-fear/